I0407508

The More Things Change
The More
They Stay the Same

Dr. Robert Owens

© 2017 by Robert R. Owens PhD

ISBN-13:978-1542750271

ISBN-10:154275027X

This book is dedicated to those faithful patriots who realize that love of country is not the same as devotion to God. Those who know that a secular religion though possibly comforting and inspirational does not save the spirit, enlighten the soul, or lead to a re-born life.

I want to acknowledge the work of the many Historians who have gone before speaking and teaching of the public secular religion which has motivated states since the beginning of time, to them and specifically to Dr. Curtis M Hinsley whose scholarship inspired this work.

Contents

The More Things Change the More They Stay the Same

Introduction

"I Am the Lord your God, who brought you out of the land of Egypt, out of the land of bondage. You shall have no other gods before Me" (Exodus 20:2-3).

Although many things in this life can be seen as being equivocal in nature in the context of Christian belief there can be no doubt that the Almighty has decreed there should be no other gods but the great "I AM" of Exodus 3:14

In the political realm leaders have been claiming to be divine from the dawn of written history through the present day (North Korea). But, the United States of America was supposed to be different. Our earliest colonists did not flee from a society led by a "divine" king. But, they did come from societies ruled by kings who traditionally claimed absolute power by "divine right."

All of these potentates were "Christian" and their "divine rights" were sanctioned, enforced, explained and perpetuated by whichever branch of Christianity happened to be ascendant in the homeland in question. In many cases the colonists expressly came to what were to them uncharted shores seeking liberation from these divinely anointed leaders who were in reality the descendants of whichever family of brigands had managed to consolidate power with time bestowing its dignifying effect.

According to Christian historians the United States of America was founded by Christians for the glory of God. As Catherine Millard states in the introduction to her book The Rewriting of America's History, "It is dedicated to the glorious truth that this nation was established upon biblical principles: its founders were men of Christian nobility; her freedoms and liberties stemming from amazing and miraculous answers to prayer in the face of sure failure and disaster (as in the case of Valley Forge); and God's faithful blessings are upon a people who confidently placed themselves under the protective banner of His care" (Millard. P.iv).

Another proposition advanced by Christian historians is that until recently these "facts" have resided unchallenged within the general wisdom and common knowledge of both the Christian American people and their equally Christian intelligentsia. The other side of this proposition is that today the history of the Republic is being rewritten in an attempt to secularize its content and meaning.

While this controversy is not directly addressed within the confines of the present volume the idea is advanced that the manipulation of America's history for partisan reasons is not a recent development. It is instead postulated that the powers in control of this society, much like the powers which have controlled all societies, use both the reporting of current events and the recording of history to their own advantage.

The period of history considered is from 1865 through 1901. A period sufficiently removed from the present to avoid any implication that the actions taken constitute a recent departure from a golden or more pristine past. It is also intended to show, through the study of the secular manipulation of what were at the time current events, how these manipulations have entered into the historical narrative of the United States.

For good or ill it is true that history is written by the victorious. Whatever bias history displayed in the past represented the outlook of the victors of that day just as the bias of today represents the outlook of the victors of today. The core idea presented in this work is that whoever those victors happen to be the bias presented will be that which is believed to be best suited to the continuation of their victory.

This book is an examination of public rhetoric with regard to the assassinations of three American presidents, Lincoln, Garfield and McKinley. The public rhetoric before, during and after each assassination is examined. This examination is used as examples and evidence to build the case that the victors in America used that rhetoric to promote the secular deification of the murdered Presidents within the context of an American Political Religion.

The concept of a civil or state religion is common in the analysis of western Atlantic cultures of the nineteenth century. The secular religion as advanced in this paper is by no means unique to the experience of the United States; it can instead be seen as being typical of the region, the period, and the common Western Society.

The premise is advanced that the goal of this secular deification sought to perpetuate the existing elite power structure. The term 'ELITE' is used in this book to refer to those who hold the balance of power in society. Those who make political decisions combined with the controllers of the media and the owners of the wealth. This group is held to be a cohesive group with regard to social organization, having a group consciousness and acting as a group to keep themselves in power, in effect an oligarchy. It is not the contention of this book that these actions were the result of an overt conspiracy or design but instead the consequence groupthink, self-interest and class cohesion.

Government documents, newspaper accounts, memorial publications, photographs and pictures provide the areas explored. Some of the quotes are extensive; they are included in their entirety in the belief that the context of statements has a direct bearing upon their valid interpretation.

4

Within the span of one generation three of eight American presidents left office via the assassin's bullet rather than the ballot, and yet the image presented to the world conveyed the ideas of stability, continuity, and peaceful societal evolution.

As a point of departure, the following excerpts from a private diary, which the author never imagined would find its way into print, will serve as a guide for understanding when compared with the public rhetoric that fills the body of this paper. Although it is known that private persons will convey at least as much personal bias as those writing for publication it is useful to study the difference between the private and public rhetoric in relation to at least one of these assassinations. This study highlights the paralyzing effect upon the private person and the sense of continuity conveyed in public.

FROM THE DIARY OF ELISHA HUNT RHODES

"Burkesville, Va., Saturday April 15/65

Bad news has just arrived. Corporal Thomas Parker has just told Mr. Miller that President Lincoln was dead, murdered. . . . It seems that a man by the name of Booth shot him with a pistol while at the theater last night. The circular stated that an attempt upon the life of Secretary Seward had also been made and that General

Grant who had started for New York had been sent for. I called Mr. Miller from the tent and read the dispatch after which the Regiment was formed, and the Adjutant read the dispatch to the officers and men. The sad news was received in grief and silence, for we all feel that we have lost a personal friend. . . . What does this murder mean? The soldiers feel that the leaders of the Rebellion are responsible, and I fear that if Lee's Army had not surrendered that they would have fared hard at our hands. My men after listening to the dispatch turned and went to their Company streets in silence. We cannot realize the fact that our President is dead. May God help his family and our distracted country. I trust that good will come out of even this sad calamity.

Burkesville, Va., Sunday April 16th 1865 - This has been a sad Sunday in Camp, for the news of the death of President Lincoln seems to paralyze every one" (Rhodes 1985: 231-232).

The poignancy and emotions expressed in this private record exposes the reality which confronted the people experiencing one of these assassinations. This private record, meant only for the author and his family, reveals the breakdown in the continuity of thought experienced by an ordinary citizen. The sense of personal loss, the anger and the musings about what it all means shows a situation in which there is a drifting bewilderment, a distinct loss of the very stability which societies are formed to provide. The public rhetoric on the other hand is pointedly meant to convey the impression of a nation in mourning that will carry on.

Chapter One

Government Documents

United States government documents express the official sorrow and shock of the people. These documents include the official announcement to the succeeding Vice-President of the President's death and the successor's inauguration speech, which invariably expresses the unbroken chain of authority passing smoothly from one hand to another. The documents show the stress that is put upon the continuity of the regime. The quasi-religious tone, the calls for prayers and society wide ceremonies create an atmosphere where-in these public documents could be seen as sacred scrolls in an American Political Religion.

ANDREW JOHNSON

"Announcement to the Vice-President.

Washington City, D. C.

April 15, 1865

Andrew Johnson,
Vice-President of the United States.

Sir: Abraham Lincoln, President of the United States, was shot by an assassin last evening at Ford's Theater, in this city, and died at the hour of twenty-two minutes after 7 o'clock.

About the same time at which the President was shot an assassin entered the sick chamber of the Hon. William H. Seward, Secretary of State, and stabbed him in several places - in the throat, neck, and face - severely if not mortally wounding him. Other members of the Secretary's family were dangerously wounded by the assassin while making his escape. By the death of President Lincoln the office of President has devolved, under the Constitution, upon you. The emergency of the government demands that you should immediately qualify, according to the requirements of the Constitution, and enter upon the duties of the President of the United States. If you will please make known your pleasure, such arrangements as you deem proper will be made.

Your obedient Servants,

Hugh McCulloch,   W. Dennison,

    Secretary of the Treasury.   Postmaster-General.

Edwin M. Stanton,   J. P. Usher,

    Secretary of War.   Secretary of the Interior.

Gideon Welles,   James Speed,

Secretary of the Navy.   Attorney-
General"
(Richardson 1897: vol.6: 284-285).

Five weeks before Lincoln's assassination, a typhoid-suffering Johnson, fortified by two or three water glasses filled with whiskey, gave a rambling, incoherent oath-taking speech. In this speech he pointedly referred to the individual members of the Cabinet as "Creatures of the People" (Smith 1976: 63). The reaction of the members of the Cabinet and other leaders seemed to reflect Lincoln's own doubts about Johnson as the right man for Vice-President. Lincoln had been heard saying that he hoped that Johnson was the right man, while using his expressive voice, trailing off in a manner which indicated his own serious and continuing doubts. (Smith 1976: 59). The same Attorney-General, James Speed, who signed the above communiqué was heard to say to Secretary Welles, "All this is in wretched bad taste. The man is certainly crazy" (Smith 1976: 63). Welles responded to Secretary Stanton, "Johnson is either drunk or crazy" (Smith 1976: 63). Many Senators were heard saying, "Is the man crazy" (Smith 1976: 63)? The Postmaster general closed his eyes and sat like a statue, the assembled people were yelling "Tell him to stop!" (Smith 1976:64).

Finally the outgoing Vice-President had to reach out and grab Johnson by the tail of his coat and physically pull him away from the rostrum. As soon as the oath had been administered, Johnson seized the Bible and yelled to the audience, "I kiss this book in the face of my nation of the United States" (Smith 1976:64). He would have started again but he was stopped by others. Afterwards he was too confused to administer the oath of office to the new congress. The only comment of President Lincoln's was: "Don't let Johnson speak outside" (Smith 1976:64).

Following his performance at his oath-taking ceremony, Vice-President Johnson retreated to the Blair family estate in Silver Spring, Maryland, while the newspapers spoke of the "Most incoherent public effort on record," (Smith 1976: 65), and an "exhibition of drunken impertinence" (Smith 1976: 65). The New York World went so far as to comment that, "one frail life stands between this insolent, clownish creature and the Presidency" (Smith 1976: 65)!

Senator Sumner held a conference of Republican Senators and unsuccessfully urged Johnson to resign. Sumner called Johnson's speech the "most unfortunate thing that had ever occurred in our history" (Smith 1976: 66).

While these incidents and quotes were not truly representative of either Johnson's feelings or his abilities,

11

the Cabinet members knew little else of Johnson except that he was a Democrat from a border state who had remained loyal to the union. Some of them had only seen him once or twice in their lives and one memory predominated in their thoughts: the oath-taking ceremony.

Secretary Stanton had dictated the official notification to the Vice-President immediately after the President had been shot so that it could be handed to the Vice-President as soon as it was necessary. One month and ten days had passed since the oath-taking ceremony when Chief Justice Chase swore Andrew Johnson in as the President of the United States, when this was finished Chase said to Johnson, "You are President. May God guide, support and bless you in your arduous labors" (Smith 1976: 82).

Andrew Johnson, considered by the Republicans in Washington to be an incompetent yet politically expedient non-entity was suddenly the leader of the regime. In his Inaugural Address, Johnson appealed to the very leaders who had previously castigated and ignored him. The perpetuation of the government became paramount to them all. Faith in the status quo, that's what the nation needed now.

ANDREW JOHNSON'S INAUGURAL ADDRESS

"Gentlemen: I must be permitted to say that I have been almost overwhelmed by the announcement of the sad event which has so recently occurred. I feel incompetent to perform the duties so important and responsible as those which have been so unexpectedly thrown upon me. As to an indication of any policy which may be pursued by me in the administration of the government, I have to say that must be left for development as the Administration progresses. The message or declaration must be made by the acts as they transpire. The only assurance that I now give of the future is reference to the past. The course which I have taken in the past in connection with this rebellion must be regarded as a guaranty of the future. My past public life, which has been long and laborious, has been founded, as I in good conscience believe, upon a great principle of right, which lies at the basis of all things. The best energies of my life have been spent in endeavoring to establish and perpetuate the principles of free government, and I believe that the government in passing through its present perils will settle down upon principles consonant with popular rights more permanent and enduring than heretofore. I must be permitted to say, if I understand the feelings of my own heart, that I

13

have long labored to ameliorate and elevate the condition of the great mass of the American people. Toil and an honest advocacy of the great principles of free government have been my lot. Duties have been mine; consequences are God's. This has been the foundation of my political creed, and I feel that in the end the government will triumph and that these great principles will be permanently established.

In conclusion, gentlemen, let me say that I want your encouragement and countenance. I shall ask and rely upon you and others in carrying the government through its present perils. I feel in making this request that it will be heartily responded to by you and all other patriots and lovers of the rights and interests of a free people.

April 15, 1865" (Richardson 1897: vol.6:305-306).

The inner circle of the Lincoln administration accepted Johnson as the successor because they had no constitutional alternative. They actively attempted to constrain his action through legislation and when he proceeded to act independently they impeached him. The name of Andrew Johnson is forever linked to high crimes and misdemeanors even though he avoided conviction by one vote. But in that one moment of supreme need he served the purposes of the elite. He became the symbol of continuity in the midst of a mind numbing tragedy. (As expressed in the opening diary excerpt.)

This pattern is established in all three assassination situations. The Vice-President is transformed by the immediate needs of the ruling elite from a sidelined non-player into a trustworthy chief executive in a moment's notice.

The secular deification of the slain President starts immediately, "Duties are mine, consequences are God's" (Richardson1897:vol.6:306). The hand of God is readily invoked and the process of linking the continuance of the status quo with the actions of God is started.

CHESTER A. ARTHUR

"Announcement to the Vice-President.

Long Brach, N.J. ,
September 19, 1881.

Hon. Chester A. Arthur,

No. 123 Lexington Avenue, New York:

It becomes our painful duty to inform you of the death of President Garfield and to advise you to take the oath of office as President of the United States without delay. If it concur (sic) with your judgment, we will be very glad if you will come here on the earliest train to-morrow morning.

William Windon,
Secretary of the Treasury.
William H. Hunt,
Secretary of the Navy.
Thomas L. James,
Postmaster-General.
Wayne McVeagh,
Attorney-General.
S. J. Kirkwood,
Secretary of the Interior"
(Richardson 1898: vol. 8: 14).

The period of the late 1870's and early 1880's witnessed the extremes of partisanship in American politics. With the surprise nomination of Garfield in the Republican convention of 1880 a bone had to be thrown to the heretofore dominate faction in the party, the supporters of ex-President Grant, or as they were commonly known, the Stalwarts. The Vice-Presidential nomination of General Chester A. Arthur the so called "Gentleman boss" of New York (Lorant 1951: 349) turned out to be the bone the Stalwarts wanted.

Arthur was linked inextricably with the other bosses of the Stalwarts and it was said that they and their faction held control in the party just, "because no capable men came forward to challenge their right to mislead" (Howe1935:102). Arthur and the other Stalwart bosses had as a goal the nomination of ex-President Grant to a third term. They tried every type of political machination to attain this goal. Garfield as the leader of the anti-Grant forces at the convention worked hard to gain the nomination for John Sherman. For twenty-eight ballots the convention seemed unable to make a choice. Grant received the largest blocks of votes but, he did not have enough to win the nomination.

On the second day of convention the anti-Grant forces suddenly switched from their two candidates, John Sherman and James G. Blaine, to a combined effort to nominate their most outstanding leader, James A. Garfield. Garfield as the campaign chairman for John Sherman did not want the nomination. He protested immediately, "I rise to a point of order, no man has a right, without the consent of the person voted for, to announce that person's name and vote for him in this convention. Such consent I have not given" (Lorant1968: 349). The chair over-ruled this point of order.

On the thirty-sixth ballot Garfield won the nomination. To appease the Stalwart faction it was felt that one of their leaders had to be nominated for Vice-president.

Their first choice was Levi P. Morton, but upon the advice of Senator Conkling he declined. They next offered it to Chester A. Arthur, the New York political

'Boss' who's highest previous public office as Collector of the port of New York ended with his ejection from this office by President Hayes. This ejection resulted from his excessive partisanship.

Conkling thought that Garfield would lose the general election and he wanted the Stalwart faction to be free from the odium of defeat so that they could pick up the pieces and once again control the Republican Party. He therefore counseled Arthur to turn down the nomination. Arthur discarded Conkling's advice and accepted the nomination anyway, saying, "The office of Vice-President is a greater honor than I ever dreamed of attaining" (Howe 1935: 109). Conkling declared that to accept Arthur for Vice-President instead of Grant for President was, "very like taking a suit of old clothes in lieu of the English mission" (Howe 1935: 110). The nomination of Arthur can be seen not to have satisfied even his own faction.

The fact that the assassin of Garfield shouted, "I am a Stalwart! Arthur is now President of the United States" (Tindall 1989: 548), did not help to endear Arthur to anyone. Even some Republicans were heard to say, "Chet Arthur President of the United States! Good God!" (Current 1959: 462). And yet when he assumed the office the ranks of the elite closed about him and he became the highest and most respected magistrate in the land.

His inaugural address had none of the rancor of partisan party politics which had always been his stock-in-trade. Instead it smoothed over the fact that this assassination amounted to the violent removal of one Republican faction by an avowed member of another. Arthur spoke grandly of the prosperity of the country, the wisdom, integrity, and thrift of the people, and of course of the smooth and "peaceful" transition from one President to the next. This does seem a bit overly stated in light of the fact that his predecessor had been removed by a bullet instead of the ballot.

CHESTER A. ARTHUR'S INAUGURAL ADDRESS

"For the fourth time in the history of the Republic its Chief Magistrate has been removed by death. All hearts are filled with grief and horror at the hideous crime which has darkened our land, and the memory of the murdered President, his protracted sufferings, his unyielding fortitude, the example and the achievements of his life, and the pathos of his death will forever illumine the pages of our history.

For the fourth time the officer elected by the people and ordained by the Constitution to fill a vacancy so created is called upon to assume the Executive Chair. The wisdom of our fathers, foreseeing even the most dire possibilities, made sure that the Government should

19

never be imperiled because of the uncertainty of human life. Men may die, but the fabrics of our free institutions remain unshaken. No higher or more assuring proof could exist of the strength and the permanence of popular government than the fact that though the chosen of the people be struck down his constitutional successor is peacefully installed without shock or strain except the sorrow which mourns the bereavement. All the noble aspirations of my lamented predecessor which found expression in his life, the measures devised and suggested during his brief Administration to correct abuses, to enforce economy, to advance prosperity, and to promote the general welfare, to insure domestic security and maintain friendly and honorable relations with the nations of the earth, will be garnered in the hearts of the people; and it will be my earnest endeavor to profit, and to see that the nation shall profit, by his example and experience.

Prosperity blesses our country. Our fiscal policy is fixed by law, is well grounded and generally approved. No threatening issue mars our foreign intercourse, and the wisdom, integrity, and thrift of our people may be trusted to continue undisturbed the present assured career of peace, tranquility, and welfare. The gloom and anxiety which have enshrouded the country must make repose especially welcome now. No demand for speedy legislation has been heard; no adequate occasion is

apparent for an unusual session of congress. The Constitution defines the functions and powers of the executive as clearly as those of either of the other two departments of the Government, and he must answer for the just exercise of the discretion it permits and the performance of the duties it imposes. Summoned to these high duties and responsibilities and profoundly conscious of their magnitude and gravity, I assume the trust imposed by the Constitution, relying for aid on divine guidance and the virtue, patriotism, and intelligence of the American people
    September 22, 1881'" (Richardson 1898: 33-34).

In this instance a man who moments before was considered little more than a political hack suddenly became worthy of the highest office in the land. He rose to the occasion and said the right words to bring calm to the situation. The appeal to religious type devotion can be seen in many of the words and phrases which Arthur used in his speech. Garfield had not only been elected he had been ordained. The wisdom of the "Fathers" is invoked and the very fact that the President's death led to the installation of another President proves the viability of the system. When there is no other choice, it is surprising how well the choice seems to fit.

THEODORE ROOSEVELT

" Announcement to the Vice-President:
Hon. Theodore Roosevelt, North Creek, N.Y.
The President died at 2:15 this morning.

John Hay, Secretary of
State."
(Townsend 1901: 468)

The announcement to the Vice-President found him hunting in the mountains which explains its brevity.

Roosevelt tried to avoid the nomination to the Vice-Presidency. He thought it was the shortest route to political oblivion. Mark Hanna, the man believed to be the power behind the throne in McKinley's presidency, was so opposed to Roosevelt's being on the ticket that, when it became apparent he would be nominated, he said to Henry C. Payne of Wisconsin, "Do whatever you damn please! I'm through! I won't have anything more to do with the convention! I won't take charge of the campaign! I won't be chairman of the national committee again!" (Lorant 1968: 454). Hanna started holding meetings to stop the Vice-Presidential candidacy of Roosevelt, these meetings continued until they were stopped on the advice of the President (Dawes 1950: 233). When President McKinley died Mark Hanna remarked to Senator Platt, "Now look! That damned cowboy is President of the United States!" (Morison 1965: 810).

Senator Platt, the political boss of New York, the real force behind the nomination of Roosevelt, wanted him out as the Governor of New York because he was unmanageable. "The people elected Roosevelt Governor in 1898, and the bosses made him Vice-President in 1900" (Lorant 1968: 477). After the nomination became a reality Platt said, "I am glad that we had our own way," then he quickly corrected himself, "the people, I mean, had their way" (Lorant 1968: 456). Platt also referred to seeing Roosevelt sworn in as Vice-President by stating that he would enjoy seeing Roosevelt "take the veil." (Lorant 1968: 470).

THEODORE ROOSEVELT'S INAUGURAL ADDRESS

"A terrible bereavement has befallen our people. The President of the United States has been struck down; a crime committed not only against the Chief magistrate, but against every law-abiding and liberty-loving citizen.

President McKinley crowned a life of largest love for his fellowmen, of most earnest endeavor for their welfare, by a death of Christian Fortitude; and both the way in which he lived his life and the way in which, in the supreme hour of trial, he met his death, will remain forever a precious heritage of our people.

23

It is meet that we as a nation, express our abiding love and reverence for his life, our deep sorrow for his untimely death.

Now, therefore, I, Theodore Roosevelt, President of the United States of America, do appoint Thursday next, September 19, the day in which the body of the dead President will be laid in its earthly resting place, as a day of mourning and prayer throughout the United States. I earnestly recommend all people to assemble in their respective places of divine worship, there to bow down in submission to the will of Almighty God, and to pay out of full hearts their homage of love and reverence to the great and good President, whose death has smitten the nation with bitter grief.

In witness whereof I have hereunto set my hand and caused the seal of the United states to be affixed.

Done at the city of Washington, the 14th day of September, A.D., one thousand nine hundred and one, and of the Independence of the United States the one hundred and twenty-sixth.

Theodore Roosevelt.

By the President,

John Hay, Secretary of State"
(Townsend 1901: 480).

Once again a man neither trusted nor preferred by the political elite assumed the mantel of leadership amid the public anguish of assassination. His inaugural address conveyed the continuity of the regime, and the official sorrow of the people. The connection between the murdered President and God is again stressed in the speech. The crime is not only against a single man, it is a crime against ever law-abiding, liberty-loving citizen. Both his life and his death have become the nation's precious heritage.

The drum beat of America's Political Religion starts at the moment that the transition from the murdered President to his successor occurs. This drumbeat is immediately picked up by every organ of the elite from the press, to the pulpit, to the school room the party line becomes the mantra of political reality. Words that are repeated often are soon believed. As the newspapers quote each other and use each other as sources the propaganda becomes the accepted reality and the personal opinion of the man-in-the-street.

Chapter Two

Newspapers

Every age has a distinctive style of popular press. Some are more rough and tumble then others. Some are more politically acrimonious then others. But in every age the media constitutes an important component of the ruling elite.

The metamorphosis of the murdered Presidents from partisan political actors to martyred heroes reflects the instinctual reaction of those who comprise the media elite of the time in the maintenance of the status quo.

Wherever possible the same newspapers have been used in both the man and the martyr sections pertaining to each President to avoid the appearance of mere political partisanship.

Abraham Lincoln

The Man

"The election of Mr. Lincoln will be a national calamity, a calamity that will do more to destroy the comity that ought to exist between the states, and to

destroy the affection that should be entertained by the
people of all sections for their fellow countrymen"
(The Illinois State Register, Nov. 7, 1860.)

"Mr. Lincoln has been borne into power by a party
whose principles are antagonistic to the principles of the
people - whose combined opposition stands recorded in
the ratio of three and a half to one. The popular vote for
Mr. Lincoln was 1,865,840. The whole vote was
4,739,982. The official vote against him was thus
2,874,142. If from those who voted for him we deduct
the Whigs and conservatives, who merely desired a
change, and did not intend to endorse the Chicago
platform, and who if they had to vote now would throw
their suffrages in a very different direction, the strictly
republican vote was about one million, against upwards
of 3,700,000 opposed to the Chicago platform. Yet it has
been claimed, ever since the election, that the small
republican minority have a right to enforce their policy
over the large majority, to the overthrow of the
constitution, to the disruption of the confederacy, and
even to civil war" (New York Herald: March 6, 1861).

"There is a remarkable bustle going on, both in the
army and navy, by the orders of our negro-Republican
Administration, which looks as if some savage and
slaughterous (sic) design were in the wind. The

27

Washington correspondents, for nearly all the papers, agree in ascribing these warlike preparations to a determination on the part of Lincoln and his Cabinet to blockade the southern ports. Did we not consider the party in power a set of madmen, we should, at once, pronounce such rumors false. Blockading the ports would be an act of war, and the Executive Department of the government has no power to declare war - that has been wisely reserved to Congress alone. We believe that the revolutionary Abolitionists, who are now in possession of the government, capable of usurping any power that they could hope to maintain: but even they are not mad enough to suppose that the city of Washington would be in their possession six weeks after the people should understand that they had usurped authority for the purpose of making war upon the South" (The New York Evening Day-Book, April 6, 1861).

"Why is all this? It is because the old Tory party, which under a multitude of names and disguises, first resisted the independence of America, and after its Government had become an established fact, has been unceasing in its efforts to get possession of it, and after having gained possession of it, by hypocritically assuming the sacred garb of freedom, it has undertaken to convert that Government into an instrument of tyranny, and to use all its powers to overturn the very bulwarks of liberty

itself - the Sovereignty of the States. Yes, Abraham
Lincoln, a Tory from his birth, is putting forth all the
powers of Government to crush out the spirit of American
Liberty. Surrounded by gleaming swords and glistening
bayonets at Washington, he sends forth fleets and armies
to overawe and subdue that gallant little State which was
the first to raise its voice and arm against British
oppression" (New York Evening Day-Book, April 18,
1861).

"Mr. Lincoln is evidently a believer in the savageries
of old Europe, and thinks that the only way to "save the
Union" is to resort to the bayonet, just as Louis Napoleon
" saves " society in France! But he is behind the times,
behind 1776, when the great and immortal truth that the
governments must rest on the consent of the governed,
was instituted for the benefit of all coming generations of
men" (The New York Evening Day-Book, April 18, 1861).

"We repeat that we are at a loss to understand
whether Lincoln intended by the language we have
quoted from his message, only to play the buffoon, or
whether in his insanity he hopes to subjugate a free
people and overturn their Constitution, by the "enormous
subsidies" which he demands of Congress. It is well said
that "fools rush in where angels fear to tread"; Abraham
Lincoln hesitates not to ask for hundreds of millions to

enslave his own countrymen, although the most enlightened of statesmen refused to allow stern and well approved patriots to have within their discretion the expenditure of but a few millions, the country being in imminent danger of, or actually involved in, war with foreign nations. Sadly indeed have men and the times changed" (The South, July 8, 1861).

"By whom and when was Abraham Lincoln made dictator in this country? We are aware of no solemn vote of Congress declaring the Republic to be in danger, and the necessity for its salvation of suspending temporarily the normal function of the Constitution and the laws, that Abraham Lincoln may be invested with an absolute dictatorship. How, then, shall we qualify numerous acts of the President during the last three years, notoriously without the sphere of his executive duties, and some of them involving the highest legislative as well as executive powers, such as could be performed only by one invested with dictatorial authority. We must qualify such acts as sheer usurpation - audacious, criminal, perjured usurpation. President Lincoln has been guilty of usurpation's, which if the dictatorial powers assumed were not used for his protection, would certainly subject him to impeachment and condign punishment" (New York Daily News, Feb. 15, 1864).

"The Lincoln meeting at the Cooper Institute last Friday evening was one of the most disgraceful exhibitions of human depravity ever witnessed in this wicked world. It was a gathering of ghouls, vultures, hyenas and other feeders upon carrion, for the purpose of surfeiting themselves upon the slaughter of recent battles. We remember nothing like it in the history of politics. The great ghoul at Washington, who authorized the meeting, and the little ghouls and vultures who conducted it, have succeeded in completely disgusting the people of this country, and have damaged themselves irretrievably" (New York Herald, May 20, 1864).

"The country has reason to be thankful that Abraham Lincoln's ambition and arrogance had become so great that he was induced to use the power of his patronage to secure the republican nomination for another term. It was the one thing needed to secure the utter overthrow of the party that has brought all this misery upon the republic" (The Illinois State Register, Aug. 7, 1864).

"We had looked for something thoroughly Lincolnian, but we did not foresee a thing so much Lincolnian than anything that has gone before it. We did not conceive it possible that even Mr. Lincoln could produce a paper so slip shod, so loose-joined, so puerile, not alone in literary

31

construction, but in its ideas, its sentiments, it grasp. He has outdone himself. He has literally come out of the little end of his own horn. By the side of it, mediocrity is superb" (<u>Chicago Times</u>, March 6, 1865). (This is in reference to President Lincoln's second inaugural address, "With malice towards none.")

It is doubtful if any man ever underwent such a massive, sudden change in this regard then did Abraham Lincoln. The press in the North reviled him constantly until the day of his death, from that day forward the press referred to him only in glowing terms. The shift was as dramatic as it was complete he transitioned instantly from an ambitious arrogant dictator into a demigod. When he was seen as a threat to the Elites he was damned when his death could be used to solidify the Elites he suddenly is deified.

THE MARTYR

"The blow came at a moment so unexpected and was so sudden and staggering - the crime by which he fell was so atrocious and the manner of it so revolting, that men were unable to realize the fact that one of the purest of citizens, the noblest of patriots, the most beloved and honored of Presidents, and the most forbearing and magnanimous of rulers had perished at the hands of an assassin" (Daily State Journal, April 17, 1865).

"We forget the points of difference of the four years past, and think only of Abraham Lincoln, the kindly and indulgent man, beloved of his neighbors, and of the chief magistrate who has honestly followed the path that seemed best to him for the welfare of the people" (The Illinois State Register, April 15, 1865).

"Abraham Lincoln, in the full fruition of his glorious work, has been struck from the roll of living men by the pistol shot of an assassin. That is the unwelcome news which has, for the last two days, filled every loyal heart with sadness, horror and a burning thirst for retribution" (New York Herald, April 17, 1865).

"The kindliest and purest nature, the bravest and most honest will, the temper of highest geniality, and the spirit of largest practical beneficence in our public life, has fallen victim to the insane ferocity of a bad and mad vagabond, who had been educated up to his height of crime by the teachings of our "copperhead" oracles, and by the ambition of fulfilling those instructions which he received "from Richmond" (New York Herald, April 17, 1865).

James A. GARFIELD

The last of the "LOG CABIN" candidates, Garfield successfully buried the "bloody shirt" and for the first time since the civil war a presidential campaign did not seriously raise the issue of reconstruction (Morison 1965: 735). As a dark horse candidate the convention compromised, choosing Garfield because of his great oratory and spotless character. He came across as a man of the people, from humble beginnings to greatness in war and leadership in peace.

This did not stop the press from following its usual partisan course. General Garfield did not escape the ill usage of the day.

THE MAN

"If Garfield intends to give John Sherman a send-off in Chicago, he had better look to his own district. A man who possess no influence at home will not make too much noise as a delegate at large" (Cincinnati Commercial: May 9,1880).

"Garfield is a clever trickster in politics who belongs to that illustrious and fragrant band of office seekers and office holders known as 'Christian statesmen'. In

34

Chicago, he made a hypocritical pretense of supporting John Sherman" (The Concord People and Patriot: June 9, 1880).

"Convictions and conscience do not guide Garfield's public life. For his party he is willing to do any wrong which will promote their interests, or play any card howsoever false which will win them power" (New York Commercial Advertiser: September 25, 1880).

THE MARTYR

Although he only held office for a few scant months before the assassin struck him down James A. Garfield became a beloved President the moment that he died. As an unknown quantity to many people it might be said that after his death it became easier to draw the picture larger than life.

"With anguish we announce that the worst fears have been confirmed, and James A. Garfield, President of the United States, is dead. By the hand of a fanatic of most disreputable surroundings, whom it would be a stretch of charity to call a madman, this great and good President, this fond husband, this loving father, this noble gentleman has been slain. Strange that the balls of brave foemen should have in fair fight spared him for such a fate. Sad indeed is it that such a glorious being, so useful, so powerful, so manly, so excellent, should become the victim of so vile a reptile. We bow to the dispensations of God and question them not" (The Chronicle and Constitutionalist: Sept. 19, 1881).

"The gentlest and most manly spirit among our statesmen has passed away. The true patriot and man of the people, scholar, orator, crusader, the loyal husband and loving father, a simple Christian has gone from the summit of earthly ambition to his eternal reward. His memory will be held dear, equally with Lincoln, though in a different way. He was a typical citizen, an illustrious example of the best fruits of our institutions" (The Boston Herald: Sept. 19, 1881).

"The death of the President falls like a shock upon all. His long weeks of suffering served, if anything was needed to illustrate the Christian resignation, clear intellectual purity and patient fortitude of this great man, the foremost statesman of our country. By the side of Abraham Lincoln the American people now inscribe that of James Abram Garfield" (Chicago Tribune: Sept 19, 1881).

"The death of no man in the history of our Government, except Lincoln, has been so generally received as a personal bereavement. His career stands as an inspiration to the people, and even in the midst of this calamity it serves as a triumphant vindication of the land and the institutions he loved, and in the service of which he died" (The Inter-Ocean Sept. 19, 1881).

"His tragical (sic) death will render his name immortal. His memory will forever be surrounded with a halo that otherwise would not have encircled it. All Americans will grieve over the sad event. The strife of party will be hushed" (The Wilmington Star: Sept. 19, 1881).

"In every aspect the story of the life of James A. Garfield reads like a romance. Others in other ages and in other climes have risen from humble beginnings to as great a height and have fallen as tragically as he fell for no fault of his. But the pages of history are trod in vain for one who, like him, fatherless, penniless, and without friends or companions to give a helping hand, was driving and dauntless in the pursuit of knowledge for learning's sake" (The News and Constitution: Sept. 19, 1881).

"Had Gen. Garfield's career not been interrupted by the dastardly act of the assassin, there is every reason to believe that the conduct of public affairs under his direction would have been characterized by vigor, integrity, and a sincere regard for the well-being of the country" (The Daily Times: Sept. 25, 1881).

"No mourning so general and so spontaneous as this has ever happened in the history of the world" (The New York Times: Sept. 27, 1881).

Once again the partisan politician is transformed into the hero of the age. In this instance a man who came upon the scene as a dark horse candidate, chosen because the factions of his party could not agree upon one of the truly popular figures of the day. The needs of the elite to create a legend which would serve to perpetuate the system outweighed any need for reality in the hyperbolic treatment of his life and accomplishments. Suddenly this little known untried President strides across the stage, another Caesar, another Lincoln.

In his life is found the inspiration of the nation, in his works are found the example of success, in his death is found the renewal of society.

WILLIAM MCKINLEY

A leader for the "Good Times" McKinley typified a time when the United States entered the world stage as an emerging world power. The greatest industrial producer and the newest military imperium, the United

States found in McKinley a man who seemed to represent the gunboat industrialism of a gilded age. And yet he did not escape the castigation of a partisan press.

THE MAN

"Oh McKinley he is sold for that yellow shining gold, and Mark Hanna is the one that holds the notes; He can talk about inflation and production to perfection, But Bryan, he's a goin to get the votes " (New York Times: Nov. 2, 1896).

"McKinley is listening with eager ear to the threats of big business interests " (New York Journal: Jan. 17, 1897).

The New York Journal termed McKinley's first inaugural address "Vague and sapless" (New York Journal: March 6, 1897).

THE MARTYR

"His last conscious hour on earth was spent with the wife to whom he devoted a lifetime of care. He died unattended by a minister of the Gospel, but his last words were a humble submission to the will of the God in whom he believed. He was reconciled to the cruel fate to which an assassin's bullet had condemned him, and faced death in the same spirit of calmness and poise which had marked his long and honorable career" (<u>New York Times</u>: Sept. 14,1901).

"The grief of his countrymen will be universal and sincere. The nations of the earth, too, will mourn. He was gentle. He was pure in his life and charitable in his views. He had noble traits of character and was generous.

He was the spirit of peace. The happiness of the American people was his great desire. He was broad-minded, and his motives were lofty. His zeal for the country was great.

He wrought that his people might be virtuous and powerful and that they might be great in their virtue and power. He gave his life in their service. He was a man firm in purpose, but his acts were marked with gentleness.

His grasp upon public affairs was great and he was a far-seeing statesman. While he guarded and controlled public affairs, he made no lasting enemies.

A pure-minded man and a noble patriot is dead, but the world is better because President McKinley has lived. His life is a legacy of which the people of this country may well be proud" (<u>New York Times</u>: Sept. 15, 1901).

"The thoughts and hopes of every American are fixed upon the President battling courageously, patiently, for life. Earnestly he longs to live:

First, and above all, that he may not leave his much loved wife alone behind him.

Second, that he may devote his days and his strength to the program of National Duty and National Prosperity which his latest speech outlined" (<u>New York Journal</u>: Sept. 7,1901).

Here again the political leader of the nation, when he is struck down is spoken of in quasi-religious terms meant to add support to the existing socio-political system. Immediately the stricken President is portrayed as the secular demigod of the people and in effect the savior of the elite.

The newspapers, as the dominant media of the day carried even greater impact then they do today. The constant references to the continuity of the regime and the stability of the nation reassured the people that all things proceeded as they should. The assassination is portrayed as an aberration in a democracy where all men knew the freedom needed to succeed.

Chapter Three

Memorial Editions

There is no other step upon the road to political deification that is more blatant then the memorial editions. Not only are they obvious vehicles for easy publication on the part of the authors, they are also a genre of literature which creates and perpetuates myths at the expense of more objective histories. This type of treatment tends to introduce hyperbole into the historical record.

It is not only the words used in these memorial editions that contribute to their impact. The packaging of the volumes, the binding, the pictures; all of these elements combined together help to raise the subjects from the realm of the mere mortal to the heights of martyrs, demi-gods, patron saints of political continuity, and the status quo. In life they are seen to have embodied the principles which make this country great. In death they are seen to have transcended the barrier between political faction and the national identity.

ABRAHAM LINCOLN

The most popular of the early memorials was authored by Josiah Holland in 1866. This edition, like all the Lincoln memorials lacked the extravagant binding and semi-mystical pictures which became a staple of the genre by the time of Garfield's assassination. These works portrayed themselves as reputable biographies based upon active research.

The authors of these various 'Biographies' did leave all sense of objectivity behind as each approached the subject from various angles. Josiah Holland, in the work here discussed, set out to prove_that Abraham Lincoln was a Christian. Two examples from Holland's own research will highlight Holland's dilemma in "creating" a Christian Lincoln.

When Holland interviewed William H. Herndon, Mr. Lincoln's long time law partner, he asked about Mr. Lincoln's religion. "' The less said about that the better, ' the oracle snapped.' O (sic) never mind,' said the biographer with a wink and a shrug, ' I'll fix that '" (Peterson 1994: 69). Holland used the testimony of Newton Bateman as evidence of Mr. Lincoln's Christianity, when this same evidence can be seen as proving the opposite. In relating a private conversation with Lincoln, Bateman contends that Lincoln said, "Mr. Bateman, I am not a Christian - God knows I would be one - but I have carefully read the Bible, and I do not understand this book. I know there is a God and that He hates injustice and slavery. . . . I know I am right because I know that liberty is right, for Christ teaches it, and Christ is God" (Peterson 1994: 69). Holland used this conversation as the basis for his belief that Mr. Lincoln was a secret Christian who grew in faith as the war progressed.

Abraham Lincoln invoked divine aid for the nation and paraphrased the Bible in his speeches more than any previous President, but, this does not change the fact that he never joined a church and he never made a confession of the Christian faith. He never claimed to be a Christian. Holland, a Christian himself, claimed this on Mr. Lincoln's behalf.

Holland's book Life of Abraham Lincoln was released in a plain binding. The book sold 80,000 copies. Stretching to 544 pages it is long on text and short on illustration. It opens with a plain engraving of Mr. Lincoln that (like all the pictures in the book) was engraved expressly for this edition (Lincoln 1).

The book was dedicated to President Andrew Johnson with a prayer that his administration would be exactly like that of Mr. Lincoln (Lincoln 2).

> To Andrew Johnson, to whom providence has assigned the completion of Abraham Lincoln's labors, I dedicate this record of Abraham Lincoln's life with the prayer that History, which will associate their names forever, may be able to find no seam where their administrations were joined, and mark no change of texture by which they may be contrasted.

The internal pictures are few, the obligatory rude log cabin (Lincoln 3)

and also the middle class home in Salem (Lincoln 4).

Lincoln Home in Springfield

The book ends with an appeal for sales agents for itself and other volumes by the publisher. What is interesting about this is that in the descriptive catalog which follows the authors aim is stated as describing " as graphically as

may be . . . the far-sighted Christian statesman, "
(Lincoln 5).

Holland begins the book by stating what his
intentions were and what they were not. He states that
he was not writing a history of the Civil War, of the
political or military history of Lincoln's administration, he
did not use Mr. Lincoln's letters, speeches or state papers
and he did not hide his personal sympathy for Lincoln or
his policies. (Holland 1866: 5) He states what his
intentions were as plainly as he stated what they were
not. "I have tried to paint the character of Mr. Lincoln,
and to sketch his life, to expose his social, political and
religious sentiments and opinions" (Holland 1866: 6). The
table of contents is quite extensive and inclusive (Lincoln
6).

The opening sentence of the book sets the stage for
Lincoln's super-human rise to prominence. "The Early life
of Abraham Lincoln was a hard and humble backwoods
and border life" (Holland 1866: 17). This approach is re-
enforced by a quote from Mr. Lincoln himself, " My early
history is perfectly characterized by a single line of Gray's
Elegy: ' The short and simple annals of the poor'"
(Holland 1866: 18). We are told that "No man ever
lived, probably, who was more a self-made man than
Abraham Lincoln" (Holland 1866: 49).

Holland traces Mr. Lincoln through many episodes
from rail splitter through self-taught reader to prominent

lawyer. Relating personal stories such as how he acquired the nick name "Honest Abe" while working in Denton Offutt's general store. The reader is told that Mr. Lincoln was a man who was marked for greatness from the beginning. His drive and ambition set him above his contemporaries. He was talked about as a man who could master any situation and rise above any adversity. It is also stated that Lincoln was the "most even-tempered men that ever lived." (Holland 1866: 83)

Holland explained Lincoln's well known habit of telling stories, "that it would not be proper to repeat in the presence of women" (Holland 1866: 83), by the fact that this type of behavior was accepted and expected in the unrefined circles within which Mr. Lincoln had spent the majority of his life and besides he was a lawyer and "His legal studies and practice had rendered this class of subjects familiar " (Holland 1866: 85).

In all ways Mr. Lincoln is shown to have been an exemplary man. He was a father who took great pleasure in his children. He appreciated their innocence and doted upon them to the point of ignoring their imperfections and allowing them to escape the stern punishments which were a staple of the times. "He was never impatient with their petulance and restlessness, loved always to be with them, and took them into his heart with a fondness which was unspeakable" (Holland 1866: 100).

The parallels between the lives of Mr. Lincoln and Jesus Christ are not openly drawn, but, they are expressed. Just like Jesus Mr. Lincoln had a constant prescient knowledge of his coming death, and of the fact that his work and his death were somehow bound together. "I feel a presentiment that I shall not outlast the rebellion. When it is over, my work will be done" (Holland 1866: 455). Holland constantly refers to Mr. Lincoln as "This Christian President" stating many times that he was aware of God working through him, using him for great purposes.

The author also draws another unspoken parallel between Mr. Lincoln and Jesus Christ in that if all the stories were told they would fill much more space then is here available. "It is with genuine pain that the writer is compelled to leave behind, unrecorded, save in the floating literature of the day, multiplied instances which illustrate his tender-heartedness, his pity, his over-ruling sense of justice, his patience under insult, his loveliness of spirit, his devotion to humanity, his regard for the poor and the despised, his truthfulness, his simplicity, and the long list of many other virtues which distinguished his character and his career. They would of themselves fill a volume" (Holland 1866: 455). In other words in a volume of 544 pages the surface has barely been scratched in as far as relating the sterling qualities of Mr. Lincoln.

In the progressive growth of Mr. Lincoln from man to demi-god Holland becomes blatant in his language and comparisons. As a Christian himself it is natural that Holland would hesitate to compare anyone directly with Jesus Christ, but, he does compare Mr. Lincoln with the founding Father, George Washington. "Mr. Lincoln's character was one which will grow. It will become the basis of an ideal man. It was so pure, and so unselfish, and so rich in its materials that fine imaginations will spring from it, to blossom and bear their fruit through all the centuries. This element was found in Washington, whose human weaknesses seem to have faded entirely from memory, leaving him a demi-god; and it will be found in Mr. Lincoln" (Holland 1866: 455).

Mr. Lincoln was seen to have grown in the office and through the trials of the war. He was respected by the people and by the world. Universally acknowledged as the first citizen of the republic, a man who had taken his rightful place as one of the great leaders of the world. His second inaugural address is portrayed as "a paper whose Christian sentiments and whose reverent and pious spirit has no parallel among the state papers of American Presidents " (Holland 1866: 503). This address is included as the only official example of Mr. Lincoln's profundity. It is seen by the author as expressing the President's brotherly love, his lack of resentment and his

50

great consciousness of the supreme power of divine providence in the affairs of the nation.

As the end of the book approaches the author becomes more strident and consistent in his efforts to portray Mr. Lincoln as a Christian who was used of God for the saving of the nation. He affirms that the entire administration was Christian and that it was the expression of a Christian people (Holland 1866: 542). Not only was this administration Christian, it was the most Christian government of all time. "Standing above the loose morality of party politics, standing above the maxims and conventionalisms (sic) of statesmanship, leaving aside all the indirections (sic) and insincerities (sic) of diplomacy, leaning on the people, inspired by the people, who in their Christian homes and Christian sanctuaries gave it their confidence, this administration of Abraham Lincoln stands out in history as the finest exhibition of a Christian democracy the world has ever seen " (Holland 1866: 542). This sounds more like the millennium then a partisan government that was seen by the people as so divisive that its inauguration was the cause for the division of the country into two warring camps.

The Christianity of Mr. Lincoln (which it must always be remembered that he personally denied) is sighted by the author as the very reason for his success. In the following passage the long string of glowing adjectives

51

leads as a crescendo to the penultimate praise, he was a Christian President. "Open on one side of his nature to all descending influences from Him to whom he prayed, and open on the other to all the ascending influences from the people whom he served, he aimed simply to do his duty, to God and men. Acting rightly, he acted greatly. While he took care of deeds, fashioned by a purely ideal standard, God took care of results. Moderate, frank, truthful, gentle, forgiving, loving, just, Mr. Lincoln will always be remembered as eminently a Christian President; and the almost immeasurably great results which he had the privilege of achieving, were due to the fact that he was a Christian President" (Holland 1866: 542).

It is admitted by the author that if Mr. Lincoln could have saved the union without freeing so much as one slave he would have done it. His statements in this regard were too well known to have been denied. But this was not based upon Mr. Lincoln's attachment to slavery, or upon his indifference to the plight of the slaves, no this was based solely on Mr. Lincoln's devotion to the sanctity of the constitution which he felt approved and sanctioned the South's peculiar institution.

Near the end of the book the author takes the extraordinary step, for a Christian, of comparing Mr. Lincoln directly to God Himself. And by association raising the fallen President above the status of the mere mortal and into the realm of the divine. "His steps were taken with the deliberateness of destiny; and, as these steps are retraced by the historian, he can compare them to nothing but those leisurely and irresistible proceedings by which the Great Father in whom the good President trusted had wrought out his will in creation and Providence. Step by step, hand in hand with events, he worked and waited patiently, for the great consummation to which all the efforts of his life were devoted " (Holland 1866: 543).

Not only does the author compare Mr. Lincoln to the Christian Father in the perfection and execution of his efforts he also draws an unspoken correlation with the divine Son in the suffering which was the earthly lot of the martyred President. "Maligned, misunderstood, abused, cursed, his motives the foot-balls (sic) of malice and envy and pride and foolishness, he waited patiently for history to vindicate him, and permitted no smarting sense of personal injustice to divert him from his duty to his country " (Holland 1866: 543).

The arpeggio of praise culminates in the final page as a restatement of Mr. Lincoln's virtues "a statesman without a statesman's craftiness, a politician without a politician's meanness, a great man without a great man's vices, a philanthropist without a philanthropist's impracticable (sic) dreams, A Christian without pretensions, a ruler without the pride of place and power, an ambitious man without selfishness, and a successful man without vanity " (Holland 1866: 544).

The author is sure that this great example will contribute to the future growth of the American spirit and character. Mr. Lincoln's life and his death are said to be among the greatest treasures of the nation which not only inspires but was used by God " to breathe, into the nation, the elevating and purifying power of his own divine life " (Holland 1866: 544). Thus it is that America becomes the new Israel, God's chosen, through the martyrdom of Abraham Lincoln. In this way the divinity of God is transferred not only to the slain President but also to the nation and by extension to the status quo.

The last paragraph of the book is quite extraordinary for a Christian author in that it is a prayer, to Mr. Lincoln, which sums up his elevation from man to Savior of the republic. " Humble child of the backwoods - boatman, ax-man, hired laborer, clerk, surveyor, captain, legislator, lawyer, debater, orator, politician, statesman, President, savior of the republic, emancipator of a race, true Christian, true man - we receive thy life and it's immeasurably great results as the choicest gifts that a mortal has ever bestowed upon us; grateful to thee for thy truth to thyself, to us and to God; and grateful to that ministry of providence and grace which endowed thee so richly, and bestowed thee upon the nation and mankind " (Holland 1866: 544). The very fact that the book ends with a prayer directed to Mr. Lincoln as to God Himself points out the reality which this memorial edition intended to convey. The martyred President has risen from the confines of ordinary humanity and ascended the heights of divinity within the context of an American Political Religion.

JAMES A. GARFIELD

One of the most blatant of these memorials is the one produced by J. B. McClure immediately after the assassination in 1881, <u>Gen. Garfield From the Log Cabin to the White House</u>. This volume is shameless in its pandering to the momentum of political deification. The author conclusively proves that every moment of Garfield's life was but a prelude and a preparation to greatness.

It can readily be seen from the following frontispiece

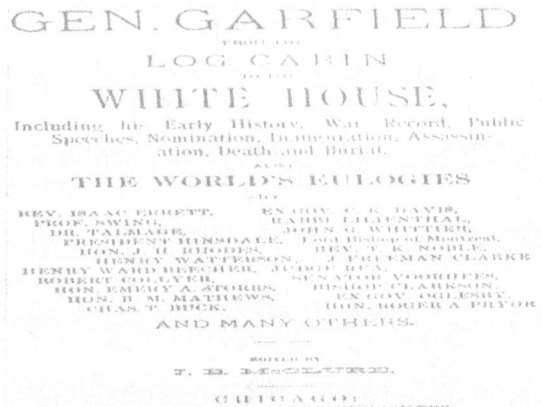

and pictures from McClure's book that Garfield lived a
middle-class life, (Garfield 2),

had a solid family (Garfield 3)

and was a distinguished looking man (Garfield 4).

The pictures are few. Some pages are decorated with the picture of the rude log cabin (Garfield 5) which was the birthplace of the hero.

Other pages are decorated with the picture of Columbia holding the flag (Garfield 6),

Eagles with the flag (Garfield 7),

and flags by themselves (Garfield 8).

Since the pictures are few it is in the text that the work is done. As a youth Garfield showed himself to be a tireless worker. "There was not a lazy hair on his head" (McClure 1881: 18). While he was a young man he worked as a farmer, a carpenter, a wood-chopper and a canal boatman. He supported himself through high school and attained a job as a district school teacher. Saving the money from teaching he paid his own way through Hiram Institute graduating as the finest Latin and Greek scholar that the school had ever seen. Teaching and building houses on the side, Garfield saved the money to pay his way through college. He entered as a Junior at Williams College and finished with the "metaphysical honor of his class - reckoned at Williams among the highest within the gift of the institution to her graduating members" (McClure 1881: 20).

After college Garfield became the Latin and Greek tutor at Hiram Eclectic Institute. During this time he saved money, got married and began to study law, he also began to preach regularly at the Disciples Church. He soon became the president of the Institute. In 1859 he was elected to the state Senate, "he was elected by a large majority, and took an influential part in legislation and debate" (McClure 1881: 32).

When the Civil War began of course Garfield, the patriot, immediately offered his services. Entering the army as a Lt. Colonel in the Forty-Second Ohio Regiment after five weeks of diligent study he was promoted to Full Colonel and commander of the regiment.

Kentucky became the first theater of action for Garfield, the hero. He took command of four regiments of infantry and eight companies of cavalry to conduct the first active Union campaign west of the Blue Ridge Mountains. (McClure 1881: 53) Up until this time Garfield had never heard a gun fired in action. (McClure 1881:54)

After this auspicious beginning there follows story after incredible story of Garfield's wartime adventures. For example when his men ran short of supplies and almost out of rations Garfield went to the supply depot and loaded a steamer full of supplies. When the captain said that it was impossible to convey the supplies to Garfield's camp due to a flood, which had a normally shallow river flowing so deep that it was "sixty feet deep, and the tree tops along the banks were submerged" (McClure 1881: 54). Garfield ordered the Captain and crew on board, put guards in the pilot house and cast off into the raging flood.

This was still just a morning's work for Garfield the hero. Later when the reluctant Captain wanted to tie up for the night, in his craven thinking trying to navigate a swollen river in the dark without lights might appear dangerous. Not so to Col. Garfield, he ordered the voyage to proceed, and he "kept his place at the wheel" (McClure 1881: 55). After the ship ran aground, the crew tried everything they could to get the ship once again afloat, all to no avail. Only Garfield could save the day, he ordered a boat lowered to take a line across to the other side. When everyone protested that it was too dangerous to venture into the flood, Garfield leaped into the boat and took it across (McClure 1881: 55).

All told it took the ship from Saturday morning till Monday morning to fight its way, against the current, in the flood to reach camp. In all this time Garfield only left the wheel for eight hours. Arriving at the camp, Garfield "could scarcely escape being borne to headquarters on the shoulders of the men" (McClure 1881: 55).

The first campaign of Garfield and his troops cleared Kentucky of rebels and drove them over the mountains into Virginia. For these great accomplishments Garfield received promotion to Brigadier General.

He then assumed command of the Twentieth Brigade and fought with Grant on Pittsburgh landing. After serving in Washington for a while Garfield served as the Chief of Staff for General Rosecrans.

Garfield gained promotion again, attaining the rank of Major-General for "gallant and meritorious services at the battle of Chickamauga" (McClure 1881: 63). He tried in vain to stem the retreat of Rosecrans army, and when Rosecrans decided to concentrate on building defenses at Chattanooga, Garfield set off in the direction of the guns. Accompanied only by a staff officer and a few orderlies Garfield searched for the remnants of the army to save whatever he could. Almost alone Garfield pushed past pursuers and pursued alike until he found General Thomas surrounded, but holding firm. Garfield counseled Thomas to withdraw his right wing, and then by his brilliant maneuvering, gallant actions and heroic direction of artillery saved the day. (McClure 1881: 64)

The glowing descriptions of "Garfield's ride" take up a few more pages. What is interesting in all this is that in most history books, the battle of Chickamauga is listed as a Rebel victory, the movement of Thomas' right wing is usually credited with opening up the hole through which

Longstreet's Rebels advanced. Thomas became famous after this fight as the "Rock of Chickamauga" and the name of Garfield cannot be found in many other accounts of the battle.

In November 1862 the Giddings district of Ohio elected Garfield to the House of Representatives. It is stated by the author that Garfield could have kept his volunteer rank in the regular army due to his "military capacity and the high favor in which he was held by the government" (McClure 1881: 66). It is further stated that he sacrificed his own financial interests and resigned after "nearly three years service (sic)" (McClure 1881: 67). Actually it took two years four months service to rise from fresh recruit to Major-General.

The rest of the book deals with various writers either extolling the greatness of Garfield in life or in death. The titles of some of these essays will convey their nature. "Garfield's Greatness of Nature, The Nation's Friend, The Crown of Martyrdom, Garfield's Greatness, Our Good President, The Man of His Time, Garfield the Typical American, True to Himself - False to None, A Man of the People, A Life That Shines and who could forget The Immortal Name" (McClure 1881:II, 51-258). Next is a comparison of Garfield and Lincoln. The entire rhapsody rises now through a crescendo of eulogies to end on the note of "A Pupil's Tribute" delivered by one of Garfield's students at Hiram College.

McKINLEY

The Memorial Life of William McKinley / Our Martyred President by Col. G. W. Townsend reach the epitome of this class of literature. The very design of the book itself is a masterpiece of the memorial edition. The cover shows a dignified picture of McKinley surrounded by wreaths and shields. The binding of the volume carries the symbol of the Tribunes of Rome and it also declares itself to be a memorial volume (McKinley 1).

The first picture to greet the reader depicts two angels unveiling a memorial stone to President McKinley in front of stained glass windows ostensibly in heaven (McKinley 2).

This is followed by three photographs which show a stately President McKinley with his books (Mckinley 3)

his former Vice-President (McKinley 4)

PRESIDENT WILLIAM McKINLEY AND LATE VICE-PRESIDENT GARRET A. HOBART

and with his mentor Mark Hanna (McKinley 5).

Now the reader comes to the frontispiece of the book, (McKinley 6) this is a production designed to build upon the interest of the times.

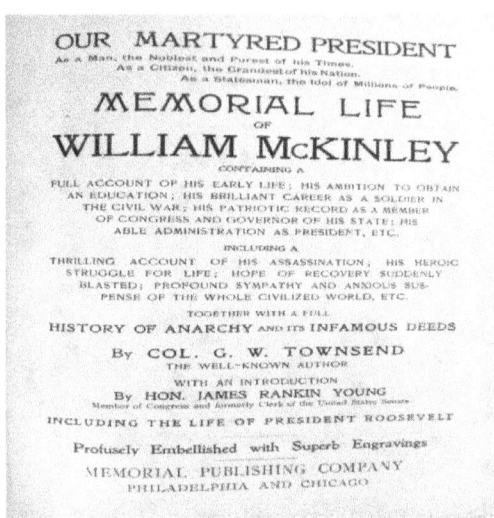

This page is really a classic, "Our Martyred President as a man, the noblest and purest of his times. As a citizen, the Grandest of his nation, As a Statesman, the idol of millions of people" (Townsend 1901: Frontispiece). The author goes on to titillate the reader with the contents; his ambitious, brilliant, patriotic and able life. The author does not stop here. There is also: the "thrilling account of his assassination; his heroic struggle for life; hope of recovery suddenly blasted; profound sympathy and anxious suspense of the whole civilized world, etc." (Townsend 1901: Frontispiece). There is a "Full History of Anarchy and its Infamous Deeds" (Townsend 1901: Frontispiece). Finally to round out the absolute apex of

68

memorial editions it also contains the highlights of the life of the new President, Theodore Roosevelt, and is "Profusely Embellished with Superb Engravings" (Townsend 1901: Frontispiece).

The rest of the pictures and photographs are of the grieving widow (McKinley 7),

the lying in state (McKinley 8),

the funeral (McKinley 9),

the assassination (McKinley 10),

the assassin (McKinley 11),

his inspiration (Emma Goldman) (McKinley 12),

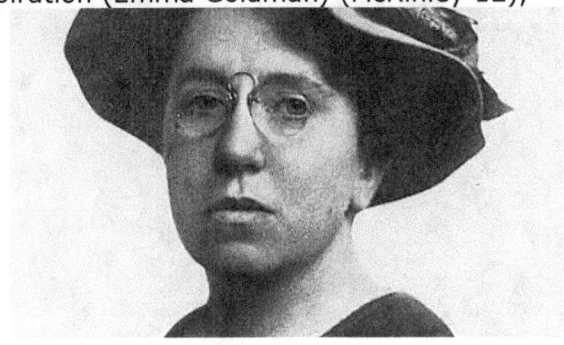

and the waiter who is said to have seized the assassin
(McKinley 13)

JAMES B. PARKER

THIS IS THE COLORED WAITER WHO IS SAID TO
HAVE SEIZED THE ASSASSIN OF PRESIDENT McKIN-
LEY. PARKER MADE A LARGE SUM OF MONEY BY
SELLING HIS PHOTOGRAPHS.

and we are told that his photograph is worth money.
One very interesting picture is the star of the Presidents,
with McKinley in the middle of course. (McKinley -14).

PRESIDENTS OF THE UNITED STATES

The book opens with a short recounting of the assassination, and then moves right into the early life of the late lamented President. As it turns out McKinley was closer to the "plain people" then any other President with the exception of Abraham Lincoln. He entered the service during the civil war as a private soldier. He worked hard to attain a professional status.

After fourteen months as an enlisted man, he was promoted to Lt. by none other than the Governor of Ohio. He soon rose through the ranks to Brevet-Major. The account of McKinley's war service is sparse, mentioning only that his service as acting commissary for his company during the battle of Antietam brought him fame for the fearless way in which he cooked the food and delivered it to the front.   After his service in the war he went on to become a lawyer.

A full account of his early life, his education and his brilliant career as a soldier fills a total of seven pages. Since this book stretches to a length of 512 pages an interesting study focuses on which areas received the greatest coverage.

Constant references are made of the remarkable similarities between Washington, Lincoln and McKinley. All three of them rose from obscurity to become the President of the United States.

He was first elected to congress in 1876 and "This sudden rise into prominence and popularity naturally gave the old politicians a shock" (Townsend 1901: 111). The entire career of McKinley from the time he was first elected to congress until he is nominated to the Presidency covers a total of four pages. The format of the book skips in and out of different time frames. Dwelling on the fact that McKinley was considered to be an expert of tariffs and protectionism, this knowledge being developed in his life-long interest in "the American people and the American home" (Townsend 1901: 128).

The Spanish-American War is dealt with in a total of three pages. The principal events of McKinley's administrations are covered in three pages.

The story of the assassination covers twenty-seven pages. Next comes the "History's Roll of Assassination" (Townsend 1901: 228) which fills the next five pages. The section on the President's struggle for life stretches for fifty-two pages. Much is made of the concern of the people, the fortitude of the suffering President and the beneficial effect of Mrs. McKinley's visits.

The section covering the honors, eulogies, and funeral covers ninety-six pages. Included in these are such examples of Americana as the "Red Men's Farewell to the Great Chief: Farewell of Chief Geronimo, Blue Horse, Flat Iron and Red Shirt and the 700 braves of the Indian Congress. Like Lincoln and Garfield, President

McKinley never abused authority except on the side of mercy. The martyred great White Chief will stand in memory next to the Savior of mankind; we loved him living; we love him still" (Townsend 1901: 301). The descriptions of the public services and the private funeral are filled with the names of the great people of the age, and the multitudes of the faithful. This section covers sixty pages.

Thirty-four pages of tributes carried McKinley into the rarefied air reserved only the deities of America's political religion. "Like Lincoln and Garfield, he was too good an American to care to be rich. As a husband, he has left us a measure of duty in self-denial to which few of us can hope to attain. A professed believer in the Christian religion, he lived more nearly in obedience to its requirements, and was more fully imbued with the spirit of the Master than is often found in this practical and metallic age" (Townsend 1901:392).

Many of the eulogies did not only allude to the political sainthood of the martyred they expressly spoke of it. The following words of John Wanamaker are typical of these verbal elevations. "The passing on of William McKinley is an awful mystery. There are millions of hearts that are overwhelmed with agony. As against the miserable creature called a man who destroyed this noble life there are thousands and thousands of men in the United States, noble and true, who would unhesitatingly and gladly have given their lives if his could have been spared, so full was it of gifts and graces, of growth and of genuine goodness.

Almost like a flash in the sky he passed on without a spot or decay or the withering of powers to the eternal and enduring. He lived and died nobly. "Good-bye," he said "good-bye to all. It is God's way." Always a sage and a soldier, and now a saint" (Townsend 1901: 396).

McKinley's profundity lasted until the last breath, and was appreciated by those who pondered his last words. "One hundred thousand preachers in 100,000 sermons could not have taught as much as these last words: 'It is God's way; His will, not ours, be done' " (Townsend 1901: 417).

The universal impact and the unifying force of the loss of President McKinley found expression in numerous statements of the day; the following is typical of these statements. "That President McKinley was a popular President was made sufficiently evident in his lifetime by his success in the political arena; but it was by his death that we fully appreciated how firm was his hold on the affections and regard of the American people. His taking off came like a family bereavement, and the universal sorrow carried with it a feeling of personal loss. The nation ceased its toil. The wheels of industry stopped. In every city and village in the land memorial services were held. In the solemn observances yesterday all sects and creeds and all earthly divisions and distinctions were effaced in the common bereavement" (Townsend 1901: 421).

The book draws to a conclusion with the origin and rise of anarchism twenty-one pages, the conviction and sentence of the assassin six pages, followed by a sketch of President Roosevelt and his brave exploits forty-five pages. The heroic President is dead, but, a new hero has walked upon the stage.

The memorial volumes form a separate form of literature designed to accomplish a number of purposes. They of course were meant to make money for the authors they also serve as compendiums of praise which would leave for the ages a reflection of the glory of the martyred President.

Chapter Four

Cartoons, Pictures, and Photographs

The final category of examination on the impact of nineteenth century assassinations is the use of visual arts to influence the perceptions of the American people.

Beginning as partisan political figures the murdered Presidents experienced the give and take of the journalistic style of their respective age. The occasion of their murders, while the cause of national trauma, became the opportunity to add new icons to the constellation of America's political religion.

The first set of pictures examined is an example of the art of political cartoons. Many times these cartoons can express both subtle and blatant themes of political discussion at the same time.

In the campaign of 1880 there were no great issues dividing the parties or the candidates and so the characters of the nominees became the battleground of the day. Picture 1 shows James Garfield about to be married to Uncle Sam when the Democratic chairman interrupts the service with the supposed illegitimate child of the "Credit Mobilier" baby. The Credit Mobilier scandal dated from the days of President Grant's second term. This was a company that meant to divert profits away

from the construction of the Union Pacific. The directors of this scheme did not want Congress to interfere so they gave large blocks of stock with influential men. (Morison 1965:730)
(Picture One)

The Democrats attempted to paint Garfield with the brush of scandal for having allegedly accepted $329.00 as a bribe. The faces of the bride's maids and the witnesses all were those of prominent politicians of the age. At the wedding the Minister performing the ceremony is the ballot box. In a time when the moral atmosphere of the nation looked askance at illegitimate children, the connotation of interrupting a wedding because of the need to explain such a child carried a stigma that needed no explanation beyond the visual.

The impact of cartoons such as this is based upon the inherent sensibilities of the population.

The next three pictures that will be examined deal with William McKinley and three separate relationships in the public perception of his political career.

The first picture shows poor confused Uncle Sam sitting idly by while big fat Monopoly walks in the front door of the White House. While only asking one question, "What will happen when McKinley becomes President?" and making no statements at all this cartoon contains a powerful attack against the Republicans and McKinley by implying that the monopolies controlled them. (Picture Two)

This cartoon is telling people that if McKinley gained the victory the monopolistic capitalists would have ready access to the seats of power while Uncle Sam, as the representative of the people, is sidelined on the porch.

One of the accusations that the Democrats brought against the Republican ticket in 1900 had to do with the fact that the extremely popular Theodore Roosevelt overshadowed the more reserved McKinley in many people's minds. The next cartoon under examination played upon these thoughts. The magnification of Roosevelt diminishes McKinley in the estimation of all who see the picture. (Picture Three)

Another perception of the voting public that the opponents of McKinley attempted to portray and exploit within the venue of the political cartoon concerned the relationship between President McKinley and Senator Mark Hanna. Mark Hanna served as McKinley's campaign manager and confidant. Their opponents consistently portrayed Senator Hanna as the puppet master and McKinley as the puppet. In this cartoon Senator Hanna who always appeared as a rich plutocrat and tool of the monopolies is instructing McKinley that, contrary to the principled stand of Henry Clay, "It's better to be President then to be right!" (Picture Four).

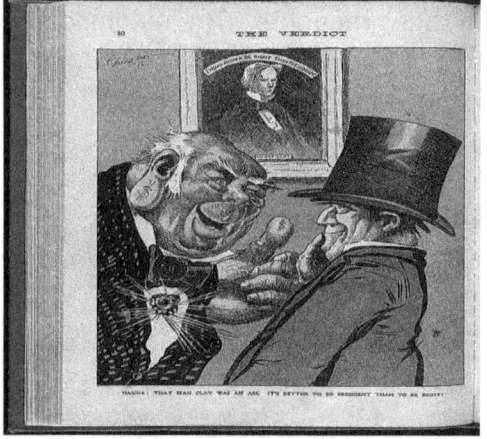

Though blatant in appearance this cartoon carries many subtle messages. It says that McKinley who looks like the Mad Hatter in Alice in Wonderland played the fool to Hanna's controlling influence. It also says that both McKinley and Hanna put success and power above convictions.

In the examples shown here the Presidents had not yet gone through the metamorphosis from political contender to martyred demi-god.

The family has always been honored in American thought. It is not surprising then that as part of the process of deification the heroes are pictured with their families. Two examples of this type are provided. The first shows President Garfield with his wife, his mother, who has a Bible open on her lap, and his children. (Picture Five)

On the wall in the background the pictures of Washington and Lincoln represent the stellar heights to which Garfield has now ascended.

The following picture of President Lincoln and his family portrays them in Washington; the seat of power. Lincoln has a Bible open on his lap and is apparently instructing one of his children in the ways of the Lord. Mrs. Lincoln is holding a rose; the time honored symbol of beauty and purity. (Picture Six)

These family pictures serve to connect the fallen Presidents with everyone who honors the family and also to place them squarely in the midst of American life. Family is the symbol of the enduring continuance of the human race. Though the leader is gone, he has left a mark upon the world, his name will be eternal.

Washington, the father of the nation, is the ultimate symbol of American greatness. To be associated with Washington is to be raised from the earthly to the sublime. In the next group of pictures examined Lincoln is not only associated with Washington, he has become his equal.

In the first picture examined standing in front of the altar of liberty are the dual monarchs of American political religion, Washington the father and Lincoln the savior of the country. The two are shaking hands as Washington welcomes Lincoln to the heights of worship, his hand raised in greetings. Lincoln holds a scroll in his hand reminiscent of the scroll of seven seals that only the lamb could open. (Picture Seven)

Columbia crowns her two noblest sons (Picture 8) Washington and Lincoln, with the laurel wreaths of champions. (Picture Eight)

Columbia's noblest Sons

The cameos of the Presidents are surrounded by representations of their accomplishments. Washington won the revolutionary war and is flanked by pictures indicative of that, including the surrender of the British. Lincoln is shown to have stilled the cannons of war, freed the slaves and promoted the industrialization of America. Columbia is backed by American flags and stands upon a lion.

The two final pictures in this series comprise one thought, the ascension of both Washington and Lincoln into heaven. (Pictures Nine & Ten)

Only the heads have been changed, otherwise these are identical pictures. Notice Columbia mourning in the foreground, the fallen accouterments of war, the beam of light signifies divine approval of the ascent of the heroes.

The final series of pictures to be examined shows the commercial realities of attempting to cash in on the worshipful need for icons. Engravers could not be stopped by the fact that they didn't have any pictures of Lincoln available. They simply would manufacture them.

The first example of the visual substitution shows a picture of Francis Preston Blair Jr. The head of President Lincoln is placed on the body of Mr. Blair. (Pictures Eleven & Twelve)

It didn't matter what the person in the original picture believed in or stood for, the nation needed icons and the engravers needed money. The next example shows none other than John C. Calhoun, the "blood and thunder" supporter of slavery as the vehicle for another Lincoln head. (Picture Thirteen)

In this instance the engraver went to more trouble than merely exchanging heads. While not visible in this reprint, the words "Union" and "Constitution" are written on the papers directly beneath Lincoln's hand, and the words "Proclamation of Freedom" adorns a paper further back.

It almost seems as if anyone who wore a waistcoat and a little black tie was open territory for the Lincoln's head transplant operation. The following picture shows President Lincoln's head riding the body of President Martin Van Buren. (Picture Fourteen)

The "fake" pictures conclude with President Lincoln in his Masonic regalia. (Picture Fifteen)

The only problem is that President Lincoln never joined the Masonic order and therefore would never have worn this outfit.

The entire category of "fake" pictures points up the need of the American people for representations of their martyred political heroes. If there had not been a market for these pictures they never would have been produced. It also points out the desire for these pictures in that most of them are so bad, the fact that they sold at all means people put their eagerness for acquisition above their discernment.

Conclusion

Col. Elisha Rohdes, writing at the time of Lincoln's assassination did not write for public consumption. He instead wrote his personal feelings and observations for reasons of his own. His statements reveal the fact that the common man was confused and almost paralyzed by the event. "What does this murder mean?" "We cannot realize that our President is dead." "The news of President Lincoln's death seems to paralyze everyone." "We cannot realize yet that he is dead" (Rhodes 1985: 231-232). These terse entries convey something of the bewilderment and pain that the average American felt when the first Presidential assassination had just occurred.

In comparison the official party line of the ruling elite soon took control of the situation. The government passed smoothly from the hands of the chosen to the hands of the expedient with no appreciable interruption. The drumbeat of secular deification began immediately and has been repeated incessantly ever since. From newspaper to textbook, from memorials to pictures, and photographs one message goes out across the land and the years; "The President died, the President lives" (New York Times Sept. 16, 1901)

Three times within the span of one generation the bullet instead of the ballot decided who would be the President of the United States. While this could easily have been interpreted as signs of discontent with the prevailing socio-political order it instead became the opportunity for the reaffirmation of that very socio-political order. The bitter partisan strife which marks American politics didn't spare any of the three Presidents examined in this book.

Each man met their opponents fairly on the field ideas. They gave as well as received in the battle for public support. All of them were undoubtedly the consummate politicians of their times. Each of them reached the pinnacle of power. Yet at the heart of the matter they remained mere men. They were certainly more successful than their contemporaries, but none the less still men. The fact that they left this life via the assassin's bullet is the sole reason that they underwent the secular deification process.

The elite needed them more than ever. To declare that there might be problems with the American socio-political structure that could cause these multiple assassinations would be to admit that these problems needed solving. And that could conceivably mean hardship or even the loss of power to the elite.

No elite will voluntarily relinquish power. The American elite is no exception to that rule. So instead of admitting that there were problems in American society, these assassinations had to have other causes.

It became the work of the enemy in the case of Lincoln. Therefore what was needed was for the country to pull together and punish the defeated South. In the cases of Garfield and McKinley the assassinations had to be the work of insane people. Who else would be dissatisfied with the earthly paradise known as the United States?

The lives of the martyrs were transformed into the epic tales of heroes. The fortitude with which they met their end inspires everyone to bear their burden. Their rise from obscurity to the pinnacle of power reaffirms the mobility possible in a free society which is based upon the principles of opportunity and equality for all.

It is the author's belief that the existence of an American Political Religion is starkly revealed in this examination of nineteenth century Presidential assassinations. The impact of this Political Religion on the socio-political realities within the United States can be seen in the continuation of the system itself and the continuing reverence accorded the martyred leaders of the past.

The most glaring instance of Christian authors shaping what was to them current events which were becoming history, an example that is now sighted as a case study in modern historical revisionism, is the work of Josiah Holland in creating the 'Christian' Lincoln. Even though it can be seen in an impartial examination of the very texts used by Holland to prove that Lincoln was a Christian that Lincoln was declaring himself to be the very opposite. The champions who wish to revise the revisionists continue to quote the adulterated Holland texts when the entire statements are to be found elsewhere.

The manipulation of perspective upon the current events of the past, as presented by the Elite, have become the history of today.
Just as the current presentations of "News" will ultimately become the history of the future. And while the individual victors may change the purpose of these manipulations has been and will continue to be the exaltation of the victorious, which as all Christians agree is at variance with the singular exaltation of the Almighty, which is His command.

"I Am the Lord your God, who brought you out of the land of Egypt, out of the land of bondage. You shall have no other gods before Me " (Exodus 20:2-3).

If there is in fact an American Political Religion what are its tenets? Upon what does it stand?

There is the creed, "Freedom with Liberty and Justice for All." There is the high priesthood, the Elite. There are the alter boys, the media. There is a Paradise, The United States of America. There are the heroes and demi-gods, the Founding Fathers, Lincoln, Garfield, McKinley, (Kennedy?). And there are the humble worshippers, the citizens.

This examination of nineteenth century presidential assassinations could easily be expanded to include the lone assassination of the twentieth. It is believed by the author that the same general patterns have been followed there-in.

The problem with all political religions is that sooner or later it becomes evident the great golden statue has feet of clay.

May the motto of the United States, "In God We Trust" always be more than just a motto, may it be the heartfelt cry of all Americans.

Bibliography

Books:

1. Current, Richard N., T. Harry Williams, Frank Freidel 1963.
    American History: A Survey . New York: Alfred A. Knoph.
2. Dawes, Charles G. 1950. _A Journal of the McKinley Years_ .
    Chicago: The Lakeside Press.
3. Holland, Josiah G. 1866. _Life of Abraham Lincoln_. Springfield:
    The Republican Press.
4. Howe, George F. 1935. _Chester A. Arthur_ . New York: Frederick Ungar Publishing Co.
5. Lorant, Stefan 1968. _The Glorious Burden_ . New York:
    Harper & Row, Publishers.
6. McClure, J.B. 1881. _Gen Garfield From the Log Cabin to the_
    White House. Chicago: Rhodes & McClure, Publishers.

7. Millard, Catherine 1991. _The Rewriting of America's History_. Camp
        Hill, PA: Horizon House Publishers.
8. Morison, Samuel Eliot 1965. _The Oxford History of the American_
        People. New York: Oxford University Press.
9. Peterson, Merrill D. 1994. _Lincoln in American Memory._ New
        York: Oxford University Press.
10. Peterson, Eugene H., 2005. _The Message_ Colorado Springs:
        NavPress
11. Rhodes, Robert Hunt ed. 1985. _All For The Union_ . New York:
        Orion Books.
12. Richardson, James D. 1898. _Messages and Papers of the_
        Presidents. Washington: Government Printing Office.
13. Smith, Gene 1976. _High Crimes & Misdemeanors_ . New York:
        William Morrow and Company, Inc.
14. Tindall, George B., David E. Shi 1989. _America._ New York:
        W.W. Norton & Company.
15. Townsend, G.W. 1901. _Memorial Life of William McKinley_ . Washington: D.Z. Howell

Newspapers:

1. _Chicago Times_ March 6, 1865
2. _Chicago Tribune_ Sept 19, 1881
3. _Cincinnati Commercial_ May 9, 1880
4. _Daily State Journal_ April 17, 1865, Jan. 17, 1897, March 6, 1897
5. _New York Commercial Advertiser_ September 25, 1880
6. _New York Herald_ March 6, 1861, May 20, 1864, April 17, 1865
7. _The Boston Herald_ Sept. 19, 1881
8. _The Chronicle & Constitutionalist_ Sept. 19, 1881
9. _The Concord People and Patriot_ June 9, 1880
10. _The Daily News_ Feb. 15, 1864
11. _The Daily Times_ Sept. 25, 1881
12. _The Illinois State Register_ Nov. 7, 1860, Aug. 7, 1864, April 15, 1865
13. _The Inter-Ocean_ Sept. 19, 1881
14. _The News and Constitution_ Sept. 19, 1881
15. _The New York Evening Day-Book_ April 6, 1861, April 18, 1861
16. _The New York Journal_ Sept. 7,1901
17. _The New York Times_ Sept. 27, 1881, Nov. 2, 1896, Sept. 14,

1901, Sept. 15, 1901
18. *The South* July 8, 1861
19. *The Wilmington Star* Sept. 19, 1881

Websites:

1. Brainy Quotes, http://www.brainyquote.com/quotes/quotes/v/vladimir le132031.html, Accessed 9-12-15

The More Things Change the More They Stay the Same